MENTAL MATHS GAMES for Clever Kids

Puzzles and solutions
by Dr Gareth Moore
B.Sc (Hons) M.Phil Ph.D

Illustrations and cover
artwork by Chris Dickason

Designed by Zoe Bradley

☆

Edited by Joe Fullman and Imogen Williams

☆

Cover Design by Angie Allison

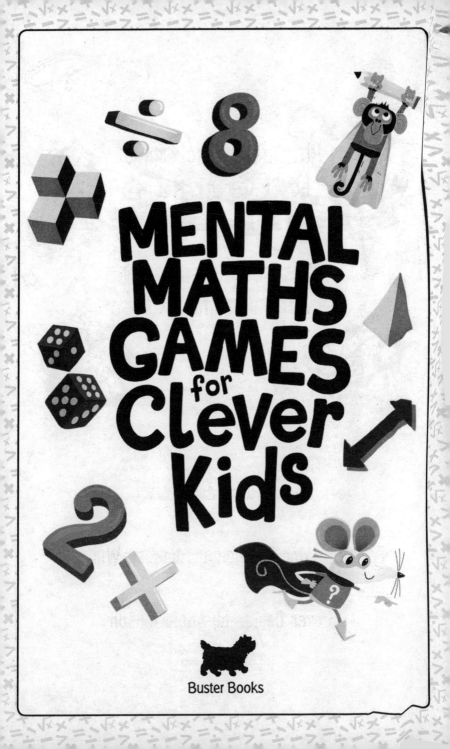

MENTAL MATHS GAMES for Clever Kids

Buster Books

First published in Great Britain in 2019 by Buster Books,
an imprint of Michael O'Mara Books Limited,
9 Lion Yard, Tremadoc Road, London SW4 7NQ

W www.mombooks.com/buster
f Buster Books
🐦 @BusterBooks
📷 @Buster_Books

Puzzles and solutions © Gareth Moore

Illustrations and layouts © Buster Books 2019

A CIP catalogue record for this book is available from the British Library.

ISBN: 978-1-78055-620-8

4 6 8 10 9 7 5 3

Papers used by Buster Books are natural, recyclable products made of wood from
well-managed, FSC®-certified forests and other controlled sources. The manufacturing
processes conform to the environmental regulations of the country of origin.

Printed and bound in February 2021 by CPI Group (UK) Ltd,
108 Beddington Lane, Croydon, CRO 4YY, United Kingdom

MIX
Paper from
responsible sources
FSC® C020471

INTRODUCTION

Get ready to go on a number-packed journey through the world of mental arithmetic in this fun-filled adventure!

In this book, you'll need to do all of the calculations in your head without making any written notes. That's what 'mental arithmetic' means — maths you do just in your head. There's usually a space for you to write down your final answer, so you can check it against the solutions at the back, but you should try not to write anything down while actually solving a puzzle.

You might wonder why you need to do mental arithmetic, when you could just use a calculator. Well, numbers are all around you. Everyday tasks, such as telling the time and using money, are all about numbers. And the better you are at mental arithmetic, the better you'll be at maths in general.

Start each puzzle by reading the instructions. Sometimes this is the hardest part of the puzzle, so don't worry if you have to read the instructions a few times to be clear on what they mean.

At the top of every page, there is a space for you to write how much time it took you to complete the puzzle on your first go. If you come back at a later date to try it again, you could then see if you've got faster at it.

If you really struggle with a puzzle, you can make some written notes at the back of the book, then try it again later and see if you can do it in your head the second time round. All the answers are at the back of the book if you get really stuck.

Good luck, and have fun!

Introducing the Mental Maths Master:
Gareth Moore, B.Sc (Hons) M.Phil Ph.D

Dr Gareth Moore is an Ace Puzzler, and author of lots of puzzle and brain-training books.

He created an online brain-training site called BrainedUp.com, and runs an online puzzle site called PuzzleMix.com. Gareth has a Ph.D from the University of Cambridge, where he taught machines to understand spoken English.

It's time to practise your mental superpowers. Below are some rows of numbers taken from different times tables. Can you work out which times table each row comes from?

The first one has been done for you as an example:

| 6 | 8 | 10 | 12 | = 2 times table |

Which times tables do these numbers come from? Write your answers in the spaces provided.

a)

| 12 | 16 | 20 | 24 | = ...4.... times table |

b)

| 15 | 18 | 21 | 24 | = ...3.... times table |

In a number pyramid puzzle, each square contains a number equal to the sum of the two squares directly beneath it.

Here's a finished example so you can see how it works:

Notice how the 9 in the middle row is the sum of the 5 and 4 below, and the 17 at the top is the sum of the 9 and 8 below it.

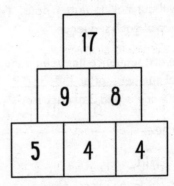

Now here's another number pyramid, where only the bottom row of numbers is given. Without making any written notes, can you work out which number should be placed where the star is? Write your answer in the space provided.

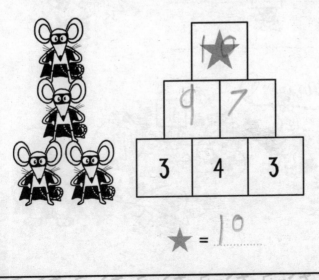

★ = 10

MENTAL MATHS PUZZLE 3 →

Can you help these superheroes work out which number should come next in each of these mathematical sequences? You'll need to use your own superpowers and do the sums mentally – without making written notes. Write your answer in the final space of each sequence.

The first sequence has been done for you as an example. The final number – after 1, 3, 5, 7, 9 and 11 – is 13, because the sequence is 'add 2 at each step'.

Example:

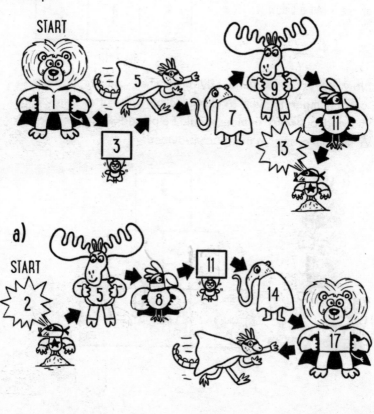

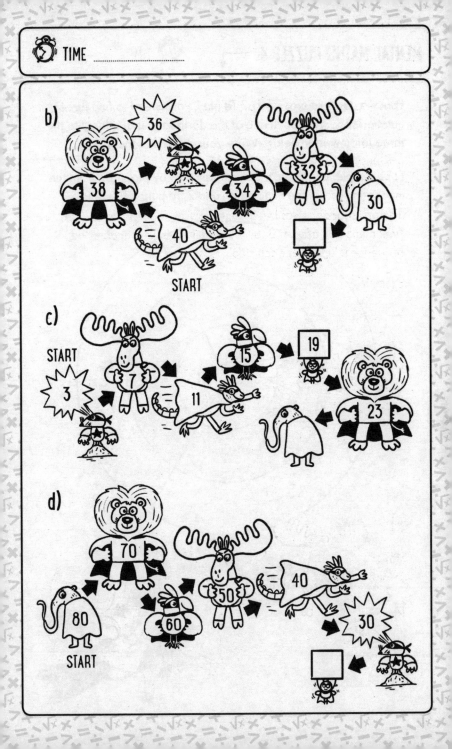

Fancy a game of super darts? To play, you'll need to find three numbers, one from each ring of this dartboard, that add up to the three totals written below. Write your answers in the spaces.

For example, you could make a total of 10 by picking 7 from the inner ring, 1 from the middle ring and 2 from the outer ring.

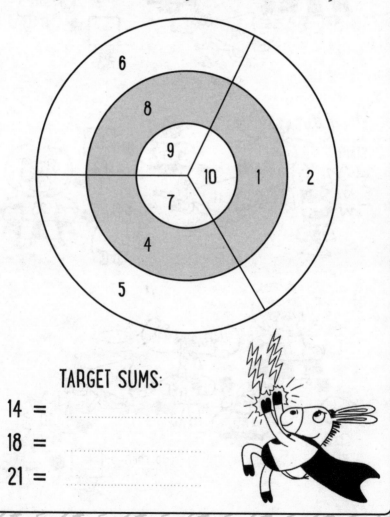

TARGET SUMS:

14 = ...

18 = ...

21 = ...

Superheroes need to have a healthy diet to keep their super powers in tip-top condition, and that means eating plenty of fruit.

Can you work out how many superhero points a banana has without making any written notes? Write your answer in the space at the the bottom of the page.

 = 30 points

 = 50 points

 + + = 100 points

A banana = ... superhero points

A superhero wants to buy a new mask, but the prices are confusing her. Can you help? Without making any written notes, can you circle the mask that has the cheapest price, and draw a square around the one which has the most expensive price? Some of the items are in the sale. You will need to work out the new prices in order to complete the puzzle.

Many superheroes work in pairs, just like some numbers.

Each of these circled numbers is joined to another number, to form a pair. All of the pairs are connected using the same rule. By working out this rule, can you write the missing numbers in the empty circles?

⏱ TIME ....

Being able to hide is a top superhero skill.

How many cats can you count hiding in this picture? You'll have to count carefully, as one of them is very well hidden! Keep track of the cats in your head, so don't cross them off or circle them as you find them. Don't write anything down apart from the total number of cats you think there are.

There are .... cats

Can you find each of the following calculations in the search grid, along with its correct answer? So, for example, for the first calculation below you would need to find '3+5=8' in the grid, as highlighted in the grid below. For numbers with more than one digit, each number occupies its own square on the grid.

Be careful, because some of the calculations might be written backwards, like the example answer – and there are some incorrect answers to mislead you in the grid too!

$$3 + 5 = 8$$
$$4 \times 3 = ?$$
$$6 + 4 = ?$$
$$9 - 2 = ?$$
$$1 + 8 = ?$$

3	1	=	5	=	2	-	9	1	=
1	6	1	=	3	×	4	6	4	=
8	2	1	+	9	4	-	9	0	1
6	2	5	+	4	=	6	+	+	+
×	=	1	=	8	-	4	8	4	3
7	×	=	=	3	=	=	+	+	+
×	0	9	1	3	1	9	5	6	=
×	4	3	×	0	×	=	5	8	6
7	=	2	-	9	8	4	1	5	6
7	9	6	+	4	=	1	0	1	×

MENTAL MATHS PUZZLE 10 →

Can you work out the result of each of the following chain calculations, but without making any notes as you work your way down each chain? Start from the first number in each chain, just below the superhero, and then apply the calculations in turn as shown by the arrows. When you get to the end of each chain, write the answer in the space.

a)

9

÷ 3

× 6

− 11

+ 16

− 3

= ....

b)

11

× 6

÷ 2

− 18

× 3

− 20

= ....

c)

12

− 6

÷ 3

+ 7

× 2

− 15

= ....

d)

11

− 8

× 11

− 9

÷ 6

+ 13

= ....

e)

14

− 2

÷ 4

× 7

+ 7

− 20

= ....

Without making any notes, how many squares can you count in the image below?

Don't forget, some of the squares overlap, so make sure you count them all. Write your answer in the space provided.

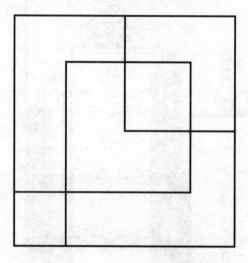

Total squares: ....

Can you conquer this cube conundrum? This cuboid started off as a set of 36 cubes, stacked in a 4x3x3 arrangement, like this:

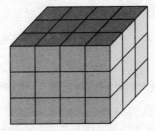

Some of the cubes have been removed, but can you count the remaining cubes and work out how many are left? None of the cubes are 'floating', so if you see a cube on the top layer, you can be sure that all the cubes beneath it are still there too. When you've got the answer, write it in the space below.

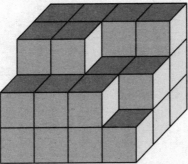

TOP TIP: Try counting each layer of cubes separately. For example, how many cubes are there on the bottom layer? Then add up the total number of cubes on each layer to get your total.

There are .... cubes

Each set of numbers below can be rearranged in increasing order, forming a sequence. Can you work out what the sequence is for each set?

Here's an example:

| 4 | 8 | 6 | 12 | 10 |

This sequence can be rearranged into increasing order to give:

| 4 | 6 | 8 | 10 | 12 |

That's because the sequence is +2 every time.

Now try these sets of numbers. Arrange each sequence into increasing order in your head without making any written notes, then write down what the sequence is at the end:

a) 15   12   6   3   9   ....

b) 4   12   20   16   8   ....

c) 41   45   43   42   44   ....

d) 45   5   35   15   25   ....

Each line of this puzzle contains two calculations. In most cases, the calculation on the left-hand side gives the same result as the calculation on the right-hand side.

On two of the lines, however, the left-hand and right-hand sides give different results. Can you find those two lines without making any written notes? Circle your answers.

2 + 3	and	7 – 2
14 + 7	and	3 x 7
12 x 2	and	8 x 3
9 x 3	and	20 + 5
7 + 17	and	3 x 8
50 ÷ 5	and	2 x 5
8 x 6	and	40 + 6
17 + 5	and	25 – 3

MENTAL MATHS PUZZLE 15 ➝

Take a close look at the boxes on these two pages. Without making any notes, can you work out what fraction of the boxes has toys in? Write your fraction in the space provided, in the simplest form you can.

For example, if you think 4 of 8 boxes have toys in, then this is 4/8, which can be simplified to 1/2.

Fraction: ....

Can you work out what mathematical operation is taking place in the middle of each puzzle?

The operation, indicated by the '?', converts one number to the other in the direction of the arrow.

For example, in the first picture, what operation could convert 5 to 15, 2 to 6, 4 to 12 and 9 to 27? Write your answer in the space.

a)

? = ...

b)

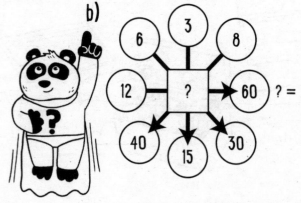

? = ...

Look carefully at the shapes of these stepping stones. Can you work out the total number of sides of all of the shapes? Don't write anything down until you've got the total number, then put it in the space at the bottom of the page.

There are a total of .... sides

⏱ TIME ....

Each of the rows of numbers below forms a sequence – except that one number is missing from each sequence. Can you work out what the missing number is, and why? Write your answers in the spaces provided.

Here's an example to show you how the puzzle works:

	1	3	5	7	11	13

Answer: 9 is the missing number

Why: Each number is 2 larger than the previous one

a)	6	9	12	18	21	24

Answer: .... is the missing number

Why: ....

b)	35	33	31	29	25	23

Answer: .... is the missing number

Why: ....

c)	4	7	10	16	19	22

Answer: .... is the missing number

Why: ....

Being a mental-arithmetic superhero means that you need to get used to remembering numbers.

Start by trying to memorize this list of five numbers.

5   9   14   20   40

Then, when you are ready, cover over the numbers, and see if you can write them out in the spaces below:

....

Can you find each of the following calculations in the search grid, along with its correct answer? For numbers with more than one digit, each number occupies its own square on the grid.

Be careful, because some of the calculations might be written backwards — and there are some incorrect answers to mislead you in the grid too!

$9 \times 1 = ?$

$14 \div 2 = ?$

$24 - 9 = ?$

$40 - 20 = ?$

$4 + 8 = ?$

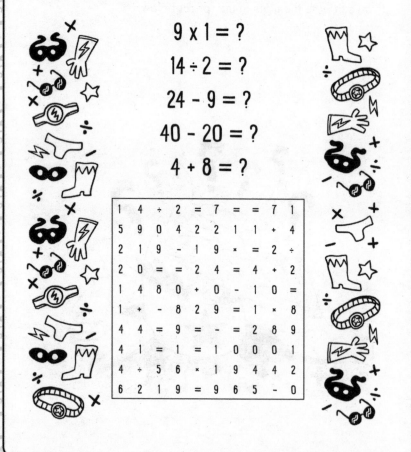

1	4	÷	2	=	7	=	=	7	1
5	9	0	4	2	2	1	1	+	4
2	1	9	–	1	9	×	=	2	÷
2	0	=	=	2	4	=	4	+	2
1	4	8	0	+	0	–	1	0	=
1	+	–	8	2	9	=	1	×	8
4	4	=	9	=	–	=	2	8	9
4	1	=	1	=	1	0	0	0	1
4	÷	5	6	×	1	9	4	4	2
6	2	1	9	=	9	6	5	–	0

Here are three numbers:

5   8   10

And here are two arithmetic signs:

+   X

Without making any written notes, can you think of a way to write all the numbers and signs in a particular order so that they create different maths calculations that give each of the numbers below? Write your calculations in the spaces provided.

Here's an example to show you how the puzzle works. Notice how it uses all three numbers and both signs once each.

85 = 8 x 10 + 5

a)   58 = ...

b)   50 = ...

Each of these heavy balls has a number written on it.

Which balls would you have to pick up if you wanted to hold a set that added up to each of the totals below? Write your answers in the spaces provided.

Here's an example that has been done for you:

18 = 2, 7 and 9

a) 6 = ...

b) 10 = ...

c) 20 = ...

d) 26 = ...

Can you fill in the missing numbers in the multiplication sequences below? Each sequence is made up of two overlapping times tables, like this one:

3   4   6   8   9   12   15   16

This sequence is made up of the 3x and 4x table. Numbers that appear in both times tables, such as the number 12, only appear once.

Here are some more sequences, each of which has some missing numbers. Can you work out which two times tables are used in each sequence, and then use this information to work out what the missing numbers are? Try not to write anything down apart from the missing numbers in the spaces provided.

a)   2   3   6   8   10   12   14

b)   4   8   10   12   15   20   24

c)   3   6   9   12   14   15   18   ......

First of all, spend a few moments memorizing these three numbers:

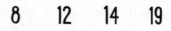

4   5   9

When you think you've remembered them, cover the numbers over before you continue reading the rest of the puzzle.

Now, which one of the following numbers would be the result of adding together two of the numbers you have just memorized? Circle your answer.

8   12   14   19

One of the entries in each of these rows is an odd-one out, as it doesn't form part of the mathematical sequence.

Can you work out which one it is?

In each line, cross out one entry so that those that remain form a numerical sequence or set.

a)   1   3   5   7   8   9   11   13

b)   1   5   2   6   3   7   4   5

c)   1+8   7+2   3+6   5+4   6+3   2+7   8+1   5+3

d)   99   87   75   63   51   41   39   27

e)   12 x 3   6 x 6   3 x 12   4 x 9   5 x 7   1 x 36   9 x 4   18 x 2

See how long it takes you to work out the result to each of the following calculations.

To make things a little more tricky, don't write anything down as you work your way along each branch.

Start at the first number on each branch, and then apply the calculations in turn as shown by the arrows. When you get to the end of each chain, write the answer in the space.

a) 20 ÷ 2 + 12 ÷ 11 × 3 − 3 = ...

b) 9 ÷ 3 × 5 − 10 + 16 − 15 = ...

c)

$12 \quad + 7 \quad - 14 \quad \times 9 \quad + 17 \quad - 11 \quad =$ ....

d)

$12 \quad - 2 \quad + 16 \quad \div 2 \quad + 12 \quad - 4 \quad =$ ....

e)

$16 \quad \div 4 \quad + 18 \quad \div 11 \quad + 12 \quad - 1 \quad =$ ....

Imagine joining all of the numbers that are multiples of 3 in this picture together with straight lines, like in a dot-to-dot, starting at 3 and then working your way through the times table.

Without drawing it, can you work out what shape this would create a picture of? Write its name in the space below.

● 2

● 3

● 10

12 ●

● 1

● 4

● 7

● 8

● 11

● 5

● 9

● 6

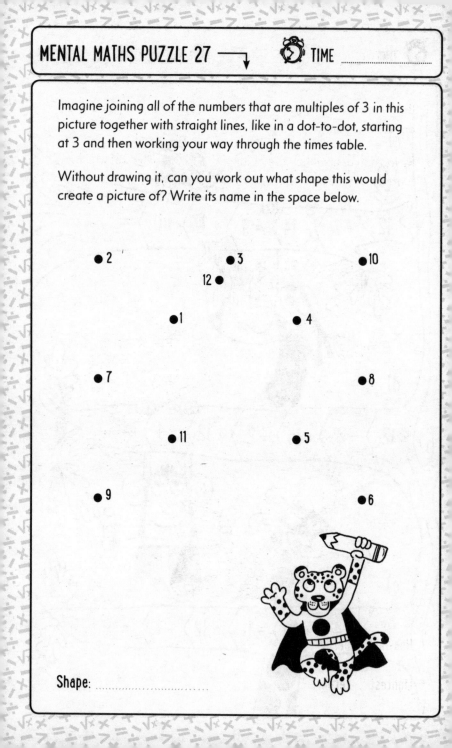

Shape: ....

Below are three large animal superheroes: a rhino, a hippo and an elephant, playing on see-saws.

By looking at how they are balanced, can you work out which superhero is the heaviest and which is the lightest?

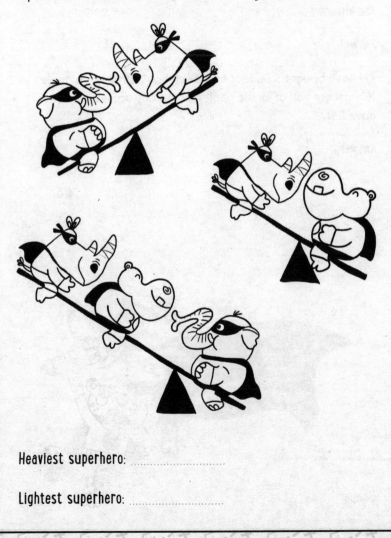

Heaviest superhero: ....

Lightest superhero: ....

See if you can write down the answers to both of these questions without making any written notes.

1) I have 5 cats, and each of those cats has 2 kittens. How many cats do I now have in total, including both the original cats and the kittens?

Answer: ....

2) I have bought 3 bags of fruit. Each bag of fruit has 6 apples. If I now eat half of all the apples, how many apples will I have left?

Answer: ....

Can you work out what rule is being used to create each of these sequences?

Here's an example to show you how the puzzle works:

| 39 | 36 | 33 | 30 | 27 | 24 | 21 |

Rule: The numbers decrease by 3 at each step

a)
| 132 | 121 | 110 | 99 | 88 | 77 | 66 |

Rule: ....

b)
| 50 | 60 | 40 | 50 | 30 | 40 | 20 |

Rule: ....

c)
| 1 | 22 | 333 | 4444 | 55555 | 666666 | 7777777 |

Rule: ....

d)
| 43 | 55 | 67 | 79 | 91 | 103 | 115 |

Rule: ....

MENTAL MATHS PUZZLE 31 →

How many cards can you count on these two pages? Be careful, because some of them are partly covered by other cards. Keep track of the cards in your head, so don't cross them off or circle them as you find them. Don't write anything down apart from the total number of cards in the space provided.

There are a total of .... cards

Take a look at this list of six numbers and try to remember them.

3   9   4   7   6   2

Then, when you are ready, cover the numbers over and read the next set of instructions.

Here's the same list of numbers but in a different order and with a new number added. Can you circle the number that was not in the list of six you just memorized?

2   3   4   6   7   8   9

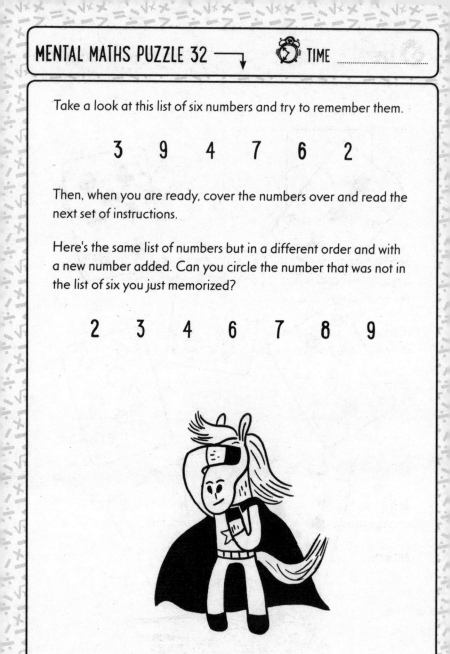

In the imaginary superhero country of Coinlandia, they have five different coins, as shown here:

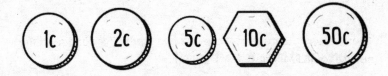

See if you can answer the following questions without making any written notes along the way. Just write your final answers in the spaces provided.

1) You have 5 Coinlandia coins in your hand. They add up to a total of 108c. Which 5 coins do you have?

Answer: ....

2) You are given some coins that add up to 75c. What is the fewest number of coins this total could be made up from?

Answer: ....

3) You buy something that costs 67c, using two 50 coins. Your change uses 6 coins. What must those coins be?

Answer: ....

⏱ TIME ....

It's time to practise your mental superpowers. Below are some rows of numbers taken from different times tables. Can you work out which times table each row comes from?

Here's an example to start you off:

6	8	10	12

= 2 times table

a)

25	30	35	40

= .... times table

b)

36	45	54	63

= .... times table

c)

24	27	30	33

= .... times table

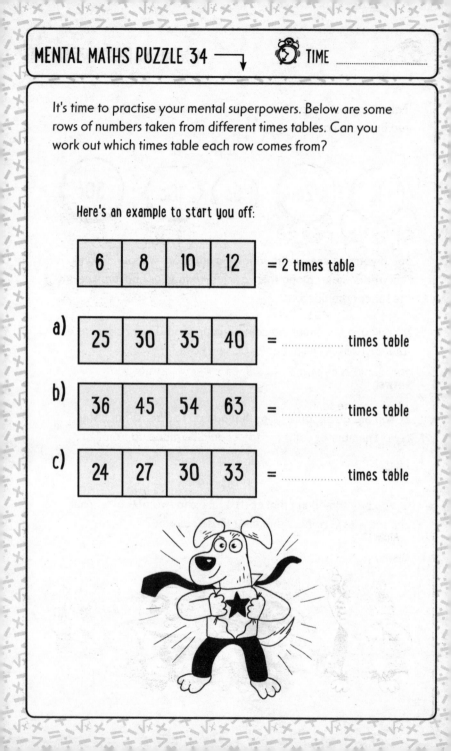

Take a look at the following five numbers, and see if you can remember what order they are written in.

5   82   17   99   30

Then, when you think you have remembered the order, cover the numbers over and read the next set of instructions.

Here are the same five numbers, but in a different order. Can you write A to E under the numbers, so that A is the number that was first in the above row, 'B' is the number that was second and so on, through to 'E' being the last number?

5   17   30   82   99

Answer: ....

Can you find three numbers, one from each ring of this dartboard, that add up to each of the totals below? Write your answers in the spaces next to the totals.

For example, you could make a total of 22 by picking 11 from the inner ring, 6 from the middle ring and 5 from the outer ring.

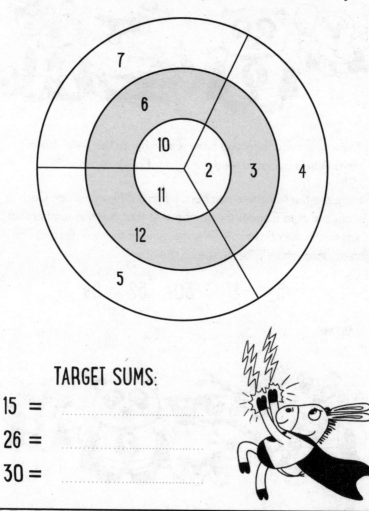

TARGET SUMS:

15 = ...

26 = ...

30 = ...

Superheroes always need to arrive in the nick of time. Can you work out these time-based calculations? See if you can solve them without making any written notes. Write your answers in the spaces provided after each question.

1) I get up at 7:30am, and spend 1 hour getting ready to go out. I leave the house for 5 hours, and then when I return I read for an hour. What time is it now?

Answer: ....

2) If it's midnight now, and I started dinner 7 hours ago, then spent half an hour eating, at what time did I finish dinner?

Answer: ....

3) Today is Monday, and three days ago I went to the cinema. The day after that, I went swimming. What day of the week did I go swimming?

Answer: ....

Just to make things a little trickier, this puzzle uses letters to represent numbers. Remember to try and do the calculations in your head without writing anything down.

Here are the letters we'll use to represent numbers:

$$A = 1 \quad B = 2 \quad C = 3 \quad D = 4 \quad E = 5 \quad F = 6$$

Now try doing the following calculations. Work from left-to-right along each line, starting with the first letter and then doing each maths operation in turn. Write your answers as letters too.

1) $A + D + B - C =$ ....

2) $D \times D - F - D =$ ....

3) $E - C + F \times B \div D =$ ....

Each line of this puzzle contains two calculations. In most cases, the calculation on the left-hand side gives the same result as the calculation on the right-hand side.

On two of the lines, however, the left-hand and right-hand sides give different results. Can you find those two lines without making any written notes? When you're sure, circle your answers.

1 + 3	and	5 - 1
6 x 2	and	15 - 3
9 x 4	and	30 + 6
5 x 3	and	18 - 2
7 + 7	and	14 x 1
20 - 10	and	2 x 5
13 + 5	and	12 + 6
18 - 12	and	4 x 2

Each of these two superheroes represents a different number.

By looking at these calculations, can you work out what number each picture represents without making any written notes?

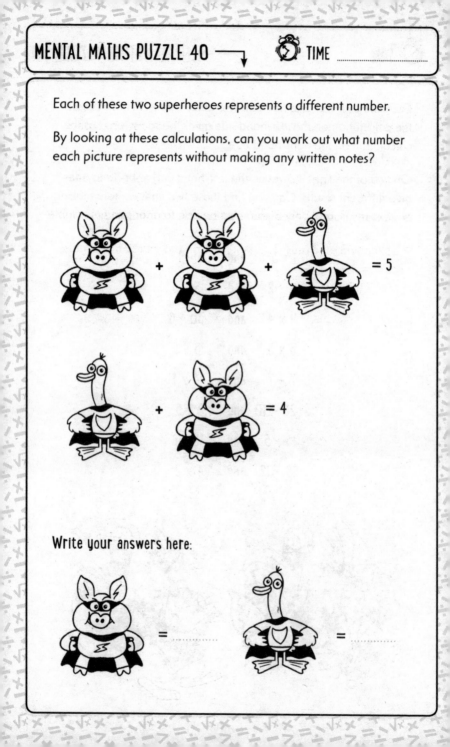

Write your answers here:

Each of these ten super-butterflies has a number on its wings.
One butterfly is an odd one out. Can you work out which one?

You know the following four facts:

- Exactly 3, and only 3, numbers belong to one times table

- Exactly 3, and only 3, numbers belong to a second times table

- Exactly 3, and only 3, numbers belong to a third times table

- 1 number is an odd one out

Can you circle the odd one out without making any other notes?

MENTAL MATHS PUZZLE 42 →

Can you sort the times below into increasing order, from earliest in the day through to latest in the day?

It's not as easy as you might think. For each time, you also have to apply the modification written next to it — and you are not allowed to write anything down!

Once you think you've worked it out, write 'A' next to the earliest time in the space provided, 'B' next to the second time, and so on, through to 'F' for the final time.

12 hours later than   **05:00**   = ...

1 hour later than    16:50   = ...

1/2 hour later than **19:00** = ...

3 hours earlier than **12:00** = ...

3 hours earlier than **11:00** = ...

4 hours earlier than **09:00** = ...

See if you can work out the result to each of the following calculations without writing anything down as you work your way along each sequence of superheroes.

Start at the first number in each sequence, and then apply the calculations in turn, as shown by the arrows. When you get to the end of each sequence, write the final result in the space given.

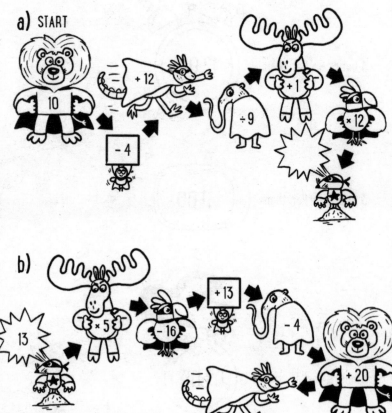

a) START

10   + 12   − 4   ÷ 9   + 1   × 12

b)

13   × 5   − 16   + 13   − 4   + 20

START

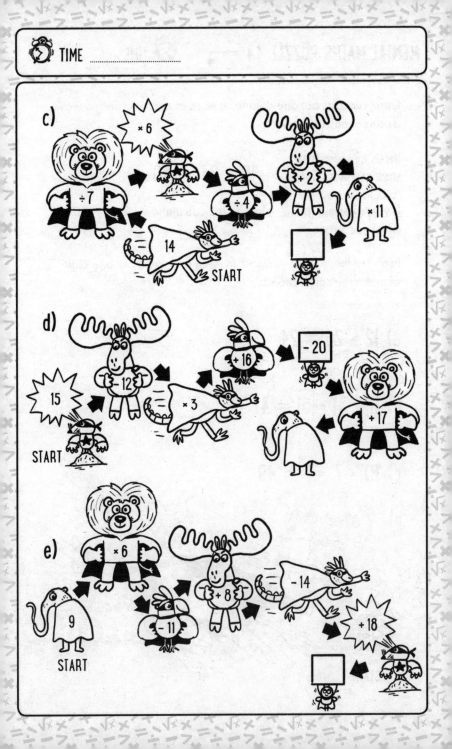

MENTAL MATHS PUZZLE 44

TIME ....

Can you cross out one digit from each of the following to leave a correct calculation?

Here's an example to show you how it works: 10 × ~~2~~4 = 40

If you cross out the '2', it leaves the calculation '10 x 4 = 40', which is correct.

Now try these three yourself. In each one, cross out one digit to make the calculation correct.

a) 12 × 26 = 24

b) 11 + 31 + 51 = 47

c) 10 × 7 × 7 = 49

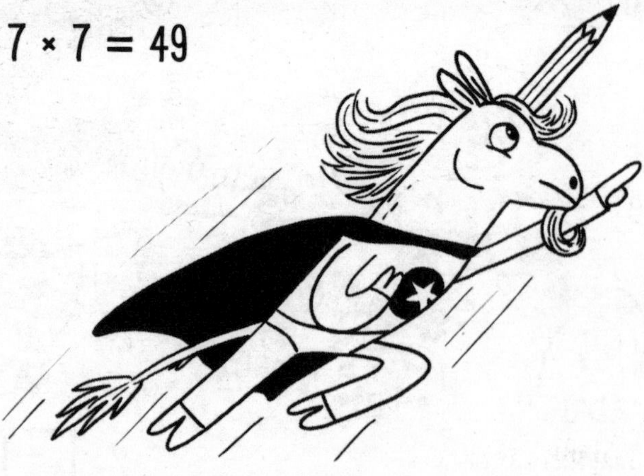

This is a fiendish mental arithmetic task for real superheroes!

The aim is to solve each of the following calculations, and add up their results — all without writing anything down! To do this, you'll need to remember the total of each calculation as you're doing the next one. It's tricky, and it might take some practice, but it can be done.

For example, if there were three calculations, and they resulted in 3, 14 and 8, then you would add these up to get 25.

$3 + 4$

$5 + 2$

3×3

$8 \div 2$

$7 - 4$

Superhero total: ....

Without drawing on the page, can you help the superhero through the maze below? Keep count of the numbers you pass by on the way and write down the total sum at the end.

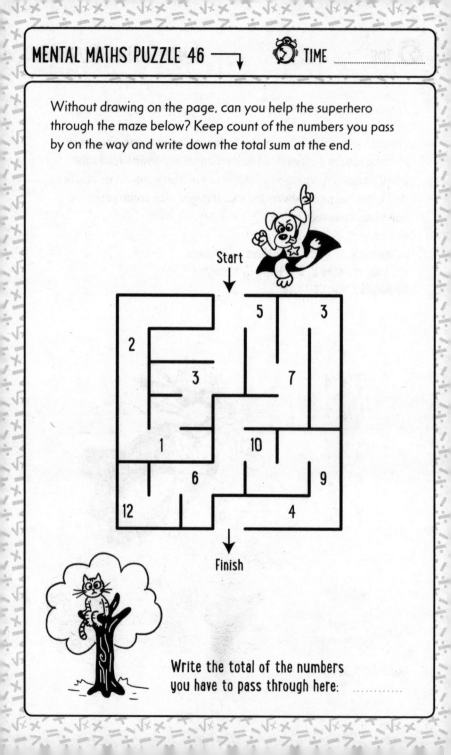

Start

2

5   3

3   7

1   10

6   9

12   4

Finish

Write the total of the numbers you have to pass through here: ....

There are seven calculations on this page, each of which gives a different result.

Without making any written notes, can you sort them into order from the lowest result to highest result? When you have decided on the order, write one letter from A to G alongside each calculation, with A being the lowest result and G being the highest.

3 × 4 ....

13 + 5 ....

40 ÷ 5 ....

9 × 3 ....

5 × 7 ....

14 + 18 ....

8 × 5 ....

In a number pyramid puzzle, each square contains a number equal to the sum of the two squares directly beneath it.

Here's a finished example so you can see how it works:

Notice how the 9 in the middle row is the sum of the 5 and 4 below, and the 17 at the top is the sum of the 9 and 8 below it.

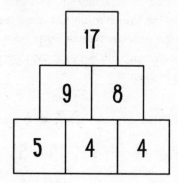

Now here's another number pyramid, where only the numbers on the far right are given. Without making any written notes, can you work out which number should be placed where the star is? Write your answer in the space provided.

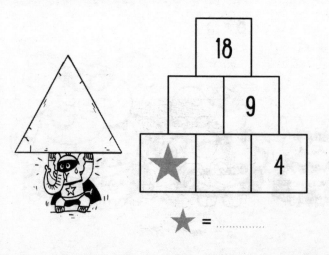

★ = ...

Each set of numbers below can be rearranged into increasing order, forming a sequence. Can you work out what the sequence is for each set?

Here's an example:

10   20   5   15   25

This sequence can be rearranged into increasing order to give:

5   10   15   20   25

That's because the sequence is +5 every time.

Now try these sets of numbers. Solve each sequence in your head without making any written notes, then write down what the sequence is at the end:

a)   17   11   20   14   23   ....

b)   61   25   52   34   43   ....

c)   55   71   67   59   63   ....

d)   56   44   68   50   62   ....

MENTAL MATHS PUZZLE 50 →

Take a look at the superheroes on these two pages. Can you work out what fraction of them are not wearing masks? Try not to make any notes. Write your fraction on the opposite page in the space provided, in the simplest form you can.

For example, if you think 5 out of 10 superheroes are not wearing masks, then this is 5/10, which can be simplified to 1/2.

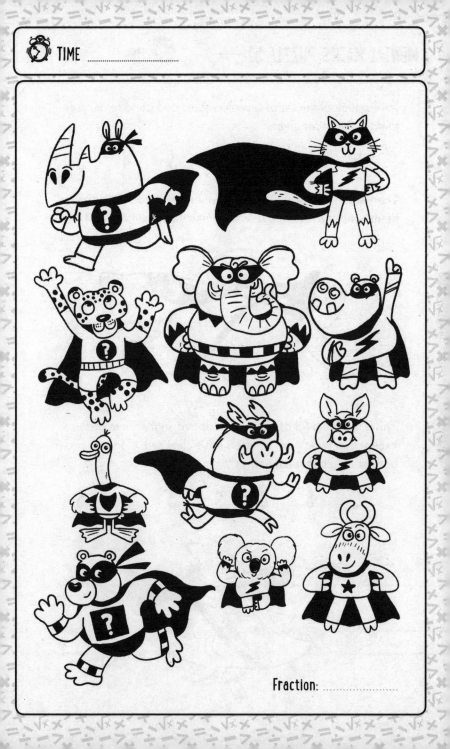

Fraction: ....

Take a look at this list of seven numbers and try to remember them in the order given.

5   8   4   9   3   4   5

Then, when you think you have remembered the order, cover them over and read the next set of instructions.

This is the same list of numbers as above, in the same order, except that two of the numbers have changed. Can you circle both of the changed numbers?

5   8   5   9   3   3   5

Each of these balls has a number written on it:

Which balls would you have to pick up if you wanted to hold a set that added up to each of the totals below? Write your answers in the spaces provided.

Here's an example to show you how the puzzle works:

12 = 4 and 8

a) 9 = ...

b) 15 = ...

c) 20 = ...

d) 25 = ...

Can you conquer this cube conundrum? This cuboid started off as a set of 36 cubes, stacked in a 4x3x3 arrangement, like this:

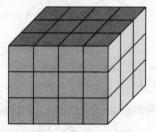

Some of the cubes have been removed, but can you count the remaining cubes and work out how many are left? None of the cubes are 'floating', so if you see a cube on the top layer, you can be sure that all the cubes beneath it are still there too. When you've got the answer, write it in the space below.

TOP TIP: Try counting each layer of cubes separately. For example, how many cubes are there on the bottom layer? Then add up the total number of cubes on each layer to get your total.

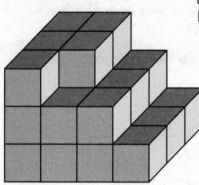

There are .... cubes

Can you work out what mathematical operation is taking place in the middle of each drawing?

The operation, indicated by the '?', converts one number to the other in the direction of the arrow.

For example, in the first picture, what operation could convert 12 to 23, 10 to 19, 6 to 11, and 5 to 9? The operation might have more than one part to it, for example x4 -1.

a)

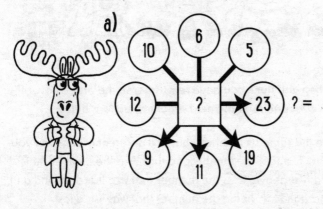

? = ...

b)

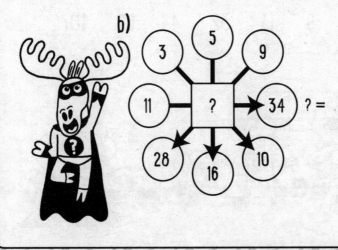

? = ...

Start by taking a look at these six numbers. See if you can remember what order they are written in.

13   44   9   107   32   65

Then, when you think you have remembered the order, cover the numbers over and read the next set of instructions below.

Here are the same six numbers, but in a different order. Can you write 'A' to 'F' under the numbers, so that 'A' is the number that was listed first above, 'B' is the number that was listed second and so on, through to 'F' being the number that was listed last?

9   13   32   44   65   107

Answer: ....

⏰

Without making any written notes, can you work out which number should come at the end of each of these mathematical sequences? Write each number at the end in the space provided.

a)　　6　　10　　14　　18　　22　　26　　..............

b)　　17　　23　　29　　35　　41　　47　　..............

c)　　19　　27　　35　　43　　51　　59　　..............

d)　　2　　14　　26　　38　　50　　62　　..............

e)　　110　　99　　88　　77　　66　　55　　..............

Without making any written notes along the way, can you work out the remainders of each of the following divisions? Write your answers in the spaces provided.

The first one has been done for you, to show you how it works:

$23 \div 3 =$ 7   remainder   2

a) $25 \div 2 =$ .... remainder ....

b) $48 \div 7 =$ .... remainder ....

c) $58 \div 9 =$ .... remainder ....

d) $67 \div 8 =$ .... remainder ....

This puzzle involves remembering numbers and then doing mental arithmetic with them. First of all, spend a few moments memorizing the following three numbers.

7   9   12

Then, when you are ready, cover them over before you read the next set of instructions.

Now, which one of the following numbers would be the result of adding together two of the numbers you have just memorized? Draw a circle around your answer.

14   16   18   20

See if you can write down the answers to each of these questions without making any written notes along the way.

1) The table in front of me has 4 plates laid on it. You place a spoon, a knife and a fork next to each plate. Next, you place 2 serving spoons on the table. How many items of cutlery in total are there on the table?

Answer: ....

2) As you walk to the park, you see 7 dogs coming towards me. Each dog has 1 person walking it, and 4 of those people have another 1 person with them. How many people and dogs in total did you see?

Answer: ....

Place your finger on the shaded square at the top left of the grid, containing the number 15. Now, can you trace a path to the other shaded square in the bottom right while observing the following rules?

The Rules:

- You must move your finger one square at a time, and can only move to touching squares.

- You can move left, right, up and down, but not diagonally.

- You can only move to a square if its number is 5 more or 4 less than the number you are currently pointing at.

15	20	26	34	30
11	25	21	29	25
7	22	17	24	21
32	27	23	19	26
27	23	19	24	31

MENTAL MATHS PUZZLE 61 →

How many superhero vehicles can you count on these two pages? Be careful - there are lots of them and they are all different shapes and sizes. Keep track of the vehicles in your head, so don't cross them off or circle them as you find them. Write down your total in the space at the bottom of the page.

Total: ....

One of the entries in each of these rows is an odd one out, as it doesn't form part of the mathematical sequence or set.

Can you work out which one it is?

In each line, cross out one entry so that those that remain form a numerical sequence or set.

a) 2   5   7   8   11   14   17

b) 5 x 8   4 x 9   10 + 30   10 x 4   20 x 2   1 x 40   60 – 20   8 x 5

c) 24   4   5   16   8   20   12   10

d) 11   24   37   45   50   63   76   89

e) 84   52   21   63   14   70   35   42

Each of these circled numbers is joined to another number, to form a pair. All of the pairs are connected using the same rule. By working out this rule, can you write the missing numbers in the empty circles?

MENTAL MATHS PUZZLE 64 ⟶

See if you can work out the result of each of the following chain calculations. To make things a little more tricky, don't write anything down as you work your way down each chain.

Start from the top number in each chain, and then apply the calculations in turn as shown by the arrows. When you get to the bottom of each chain, write the final result in the space.

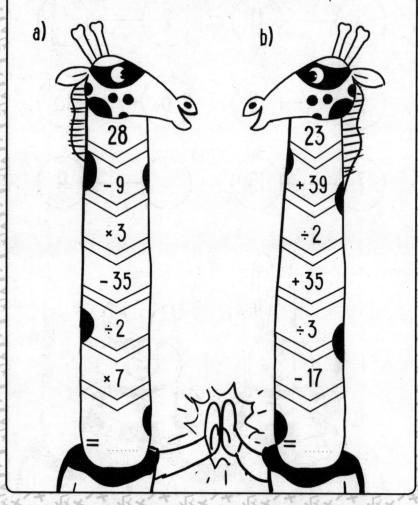

a)

28

− 9

× 3

− 35

÷ 2

× 7

= ....

b)

23

+ 39

÷ 2

+ 35

÷ 3

− 17

= ....

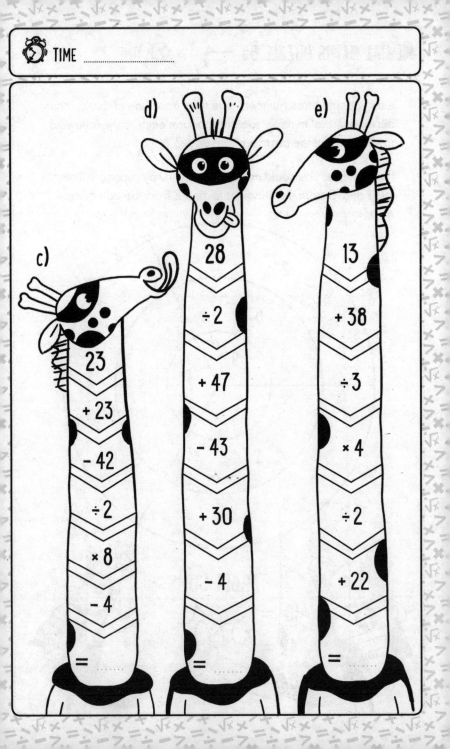

c)

23

+ 23

− 42

÷ 2

× 8

− 4

=

d)

28

÷ 2

+ 47

− 43

+ 30

− 4

=

e)

13

+ 38

÷ 3

× 4

÷ 2

+ 22

=

Can you find three numbers, one from each ring of this dartboard, that multiply together to form each of the following totals shown at the bottom of the page?

For example, you could make a total of 10 by picking 1 from the inner ring, 5 from the middle ring, and 2 from the outer ring.

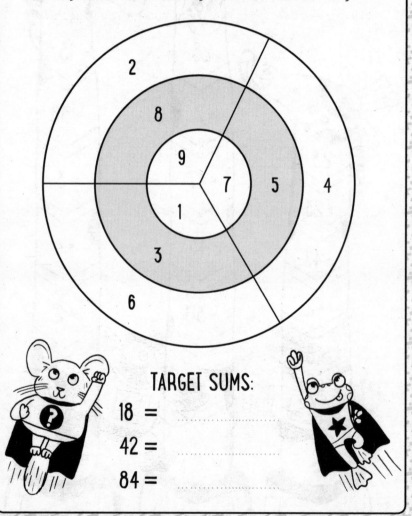

TARGET SUMS:

18 = ...

42 = ...

84 = ...

Each line of this puzzle contains two calculations. In most cases, the calculation on the left-hand side gives the same result as the calculation on the right-hand side.

On two of the lines, however, the left-hand and right-hand sides give different results. Can you find those two lines without making any written notes? When you're sure, circle your answers.

5 x 2	and	15 – 5
7 x 7	and	5 x 9
3 + 12	and	5 x 3
6 + 6	and	7 + 5
9 x 9	and	90 – 9
5 x 5	and	40 – 15
7 + 32	and	47 – 9
8 x 3	and	2 x 12

MENTAL MATHS PUZZLE 67 → ⏱ TIME ....

A superhero wants to buy a pair of boots but the sale prices are confusing him. Can you help? Without making any written notes, can you circle the pair that has the cheapest price, and draw a rectangle around the pair that has the most expensive price?

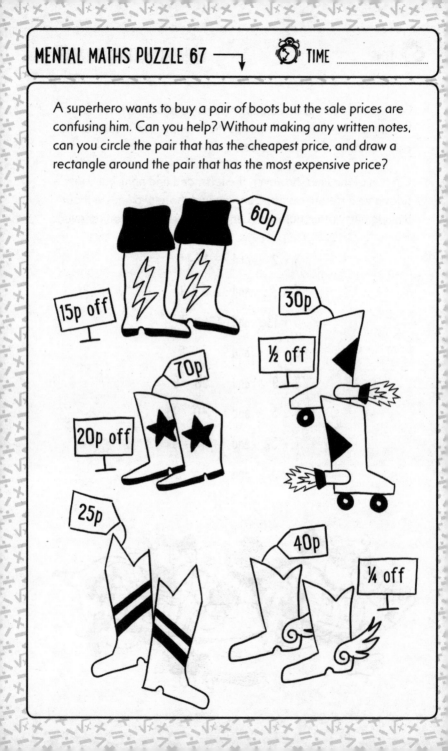

Can you fill in the missing numbers in the multiplication sequences below? Each sequence should be made up of two overlapping times tables, without gaps, like this one:

3   4   6   8   9   12   15   16

This sequence is made up of the 3x and 4x table. Numbers that appear in both times tables – such as the number 12 – only appear once.

Here are some more sequences, each of which has some missing numbers. Can you work out which two times tables are used in each sequence, and then use this information to work out what the missing numbers are? Try not to write anything down apart from the missing numbers in the spaces provided.

a)   5   6   10   15   18   20   24   ......

b)   4   8   12   14   16   21   24

c)   9   14   18   21   28   35   36

Can you sort the times below into increasing order, from earliest in the day through to latest in the day?

It's not as easy as you might think. For each time, you also have to apply the modification written next to it – and you are not allowed to write anything down!

Once you think you've worked it out, write 'A' next to the earliest time in the space provided, 'B' next to the second time and so on, through to 'E' for the final time.

60 minutes earlier than  **3am** = ...

2 hours later than  12:15am = ...

⏰ TIME ....

45 minutes later than **6pm** = ...

4 hours later than **4:30pm** = ...

2 1/2 hours later than **10:45am** = ...

90 minutes earlier than **2pm** = ...

Take a look at this list of six numbers and try to remember them.

5   10   4   7   13   8

Then, when you are ready, cover the numbers over and read the next set of instructions.

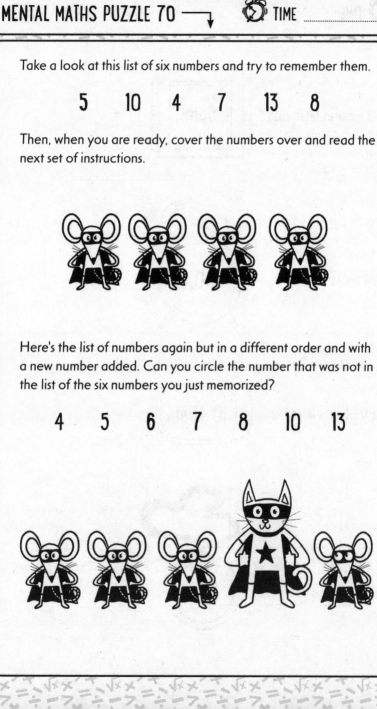

Here's the list of numbers again but in a different order and with a new number added. Can you circle the number that was not in the list of the six numbers you just memorized?

4   5   6   7   8   10   13

In a number pyramid puzzle, each square contains a number equal to the sum of the two squares directly beneath it.

Here's a finished pyramid so you can see how the puzzle works:

Notice how the 9 in the middle row is the sum of the 5 and 4 below, and the 17 at the top is the sum of the 9 and 8 below it.

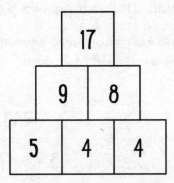

Here's another number pyramid where only three of the numbers are given. Without making any written notes, can you work out which number should be placed where the star is? Write your answer in the space provided.

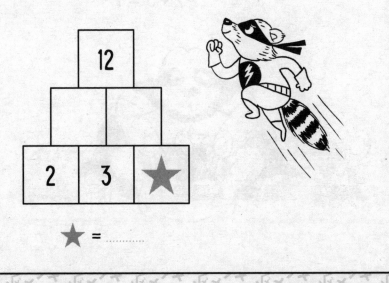

★ = ...

Can you help the superhero find the missing number? All of the calculations below are missing the same number. The number is between 1 and 9. If you were to write that number in each of the spaces, all the calculations would give the same result.

Try to work this out without making any written notes. Just fill in the answers when you're done.

.... + 10 + 2 = ?

3 × .... = ?

.... × 2 + 6 = ?

25 − 13 + ... = ?

5 × .... ÷ 2 + 3 = ?

Each of these three superhero items – a belt, a glove and a helmet – represents a different number.

By looking at these calculations, can you work out what numbers the belt and the glove represent?

 + 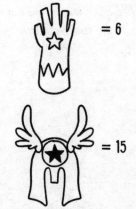 = 6

 + = 15

 = 10

Write your answers here:

 = ...    = ...

See if you can memorize this list of five numbers without writing anything down.

12   8   50   5   100

When you think you've got it, cover the numbers over and see if you can write them in the spaces below.

Answer: ....

In the world of the animal superheroes, there are six banknotes, which are shown below:

See if you can answer the following questions without making any written notes. Just write your final answers in the spaces.

a) You have 4 superhero banknotes in your hand. They add up to 56b, so what must those banknotes be?

Answer: ....

b) You have some banknotes that add up to 144b. What is the fewest number of banknotes this total could be made from?

Answer: ....

c) You buy something that costs 101b, using three 50 banknotes. Your change contains 5 banknotes. What must those 5 banknotes be?

Answer: ....

Without making any notes, how many triangles can you count in the image below?

Be careful, because sometimes the same lines may be used to make up more than one triangle! When you've come up with an answer, write it in the space provided.

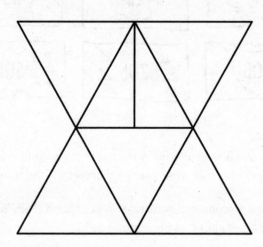

Total triangles: ....

Can you find each of the following calculations in the search grid, along with its correct answer? For numbers with more than one digit, each number occupies its own square on the grid.

Be careful, because some of the calculations might be written backwards — and there are some incorrect answers to mislead you in the grid too!

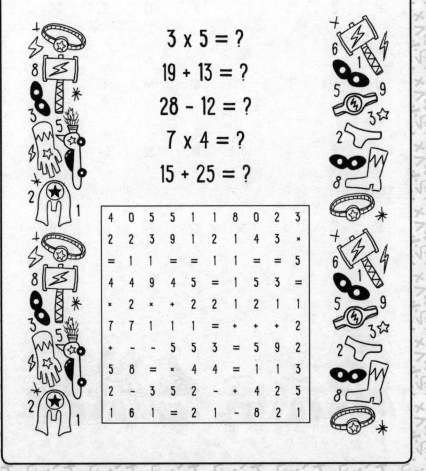

3 x 5 = ?

19 + 13 = ?

28 - 12 = ?

7 x 4 = ?

15 + 25 = ?

4	0	5	5	1	1	8	0	2	3
2	2	3	9	1	2	1	4	3	×
=	1	1	=	=	1	1	=	=	5
4	4	9	4	5	=	1	5	3	=
×	2	×	+	2	2	1	2	1	1
7	7	1	1	1	=	+	+	+	2
+	-	-	5	5	3	=	5	9	2
5	8	=	×	4	4	=	1	1	3
2	-	3	5	2	-	+	4	2	5
1	6	1	=	2	1	-	8	2	1

MENTAL MATHS PUZZLE 78 ⟶   ⏱ TIME ....

Can you work out what rule is being used to create each of these sequences? Write your answers in the spaces provided.

This one has been done for you as an example:

| 39 | 35 | 31 | 27 | 23 | 19 | 15 |

Rule: The numbers decrease by 4 at each step

a)   2   3   5   8   13   21   34

Rule: ....

b)   144   121   100   81   64   49   36

Rule: ....

c)   2   4   8   16   32   64   128

Rule: ....

d)   13   15   18   22   27   33   40

Rule: ....

This puzzle involves remembering numbers and then doing mental arithmetic with them. First of all, spend a few moments memorizing the following three numbers.

8   11   15

When you think you're ready, cover the numbers over and read the next part of the puzzle.

Now, which one of the following numbers would be the result of adding together two of the numbers you have just memorized? Circle your answer.

14   17   21   23

Each line of this puzzle contains two calculations. In most cases, the calculation on the left-hand side gives the same result as the calculation on the right-hand side.

On two of the lines, however, the left-hand and right-hand sides give different results. Can you find those two lines without making any written notes? When you're sure, circle your answers.

5 x 3	and	20 – 5
9 x 10	and	110 – 20
5 x 7	and	3 x 12
4 + 24	and	7 x 4
19 + 19	and	15 + 23
15 + 23	and	44 – 8
6 x 6	and	27 + 9
90 ÷ 9	and	40 – 30

Each of these superhero shields has a number written on it:

Which shields would you have to pick if you wanted to hold a set that added up to each of the totals below? Write your answers in the spaces provided.

The first one has been done for you to show you how it works:

18 = 8 and 10

a) 21 = ...

b) 32 = ...

c) 37 = ...

d) 44 = ...

Try these tricky time-based calculations and see if you can solve them without making any written notes.

1) I was awake for 15 hours yesterday. Exactly halfway through the time I was awake I had lunch, and then two hours later I had a snack. I had the snack at 4pm, so what time did I wake up yesterday?

Answer: ....

2) The day after the day before yesterday is Thursday. What day is today?

Answer: ....

3) Due to time differences, if it's 12pm in London then it's 7am in New York City. So, if it's now 3pm in New York City, what time is it in London?

Answer: ....

Can you conquer this cube conundrum? This cuboid started off as a set of 64 cubes, stacked in a 4x4x4 arrangement, like this:

Some of the cubes have been removed, but can you count the remaining cubes and work out how many are left? None of the cubes are 'floating', so if you see a cube on the top layer, you can be sure that all the cubes beneath it are still there too. When you've got the answer, write it in the space below.

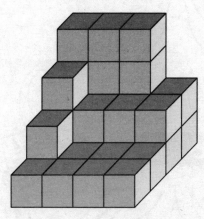

TOP TIP: Try counting each layer of cubes separately. For example, how many cubes are there on the bottom layer? Then add up the total number of cubes on each layer to get your total.

There are .... cubes

Superhero Squid is holding up ten numbers, but one number is different from the others. Can you work out which one?

You know the following four facts:

- Exactly 3, and only 3, numbers belong to one particular times table

- Exactly 3, and only 3, numbers belong to a second times table

- Exactly 3, and only 3, numbers belong to a third times table

- 1 number is an odd one out

Can you circle the odd one out without making any written notes?

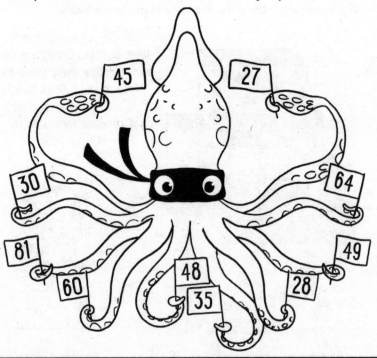

See if you can write down the answers to each of these questions without making any written notes.

1) I'm at a friend's party and they offer to buy everyone there an ice cream. There are 12 people at the party, but a quarter of them don't want ice creams. How many people end up with an ice cream?

Answer: ....

2) Every day I eat 2 apples and 1 banana, and three days a week I also eat 1 orange. How many pieces of fruit do I eat each week?

Answer: ....

Take some time to look at these two baskets of fruit being held up by mini superheroes. They are filled with bananas, pineapples and oranges.

In your head, count how many of each type of fruit you can see, then answer the questions on the following page.

1) What type of fruit is there most of?

Answer: ....

2) What type of fruit is there least of?

Answer: ....

Can you work out the result of each of the following chain calculations, without writing anything down as you work your way down each chain? Start at the top and then apply the calculations in turn as shown by the arrows. When you get to the end of each chain, write the final result in the space at the bottom.

a)
34
÷ 2
+ 48
÷ 5
+ 27
× 2
= ....

b)
35
+ 10
÷ 3
− 8
+ 44
− 48
= ....

c)

25

÷ 5

+ 1

– 4

+ 9

– 1

= _____

d)

7

× 8

– 6

+ 11

– 41

+ 17

= _____

e)

24

+ 45

÷ 3

– 5

+ 23

– 12

= _____

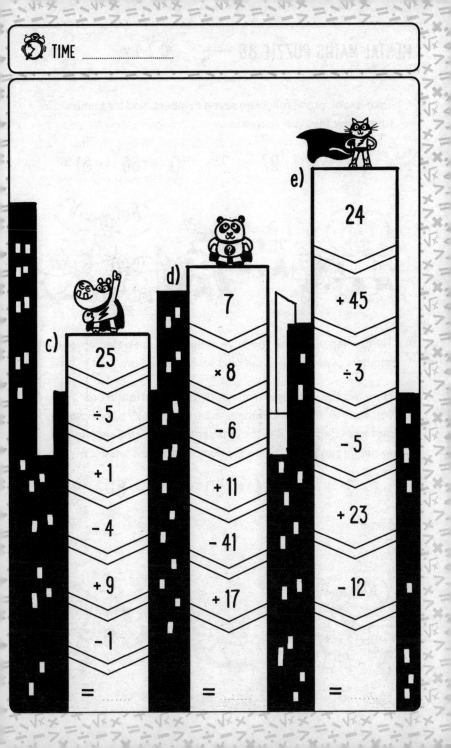

Take a look at the following seven numbers, and try to memorize what order they are written in.

3   34   97   2   50   66   81

Then, when you think you have memorized the order, cover the numbers over and read the next set of instructions.

Here are the same seven numbers, but in a different order. Can you write 'A' to 'G' under the numbers, so that 'A' is the number that was listed first, 'B' is the number that was listed second and so on, through to 'G' being the number that was listed last?

2   3   34   50   66   81   97

Answer: ....

Each of the rows of numbers below forms a sequence — except that one number is missing from each sequence. Can you work out what that missing number is, and why? Write your answers in the spaces provided.

The first one has been done for you as an example:

| 2 | 4 | 6 | 8 | | 12 | 14 |

Answer: 10 is the missing number
Why: Each number is 2 larger than the previous one

a)   73   70   67   64   61   55

Answer: .... is the missing number
Why: ....

b)   6   12   15   18   21   24

Answer: .... is the missing number
Why: ....

c)   19   26   40   47   54   61

Answer: .... is the missing number
Why: ....

Here are four numbers:

$$1 \quad\quad 2 \quad\quad 5 \quad\quad 10$$

And here are three arithmetic signs:

$$+ \quad\quad + \quad\quad \times$$

Without making any written notes, can you think of a way
to write all of the numbers and signs in a particular order so that
they create different maths calculations that give each of
the totals below? Write your answers in the spaces provided.

To show you how it works, an example has been done for you.
Notice how it uses all four numbers and all three signs once each.

$$17 = 10 \times 1 + 5 + 2$$

a)   53 = ...

b)   26 = ...

c)   21 = ...

Can you find each of the following calculations in the search grid, along with its correct answer? For numbers with more than one digit, each number occupies its own square on the grid.

Be careful, because some of the calculations might be written backwards – and there are some incorrect answers to mislead you in the grid too!

$$18 + 2 = ?$$
$$35 - 25 = ?$$
$$5 \times 8 = ?$$
$$110 \div 10 = ?$$
$$96 \div 12 = ?$$

1	1	8	+	2	=	2	2	0	÷
5	3	5	-	2	5	=	1	5	2
1	1	0	÷	1	0	=	1	1	3
0	0	1	1	1	0	9	9	5	0
×	8	0	×	1	=	6	-	4	8
2	2	5	÷	2	÷	2	=	×	1
3	5	0	1	1	5	8	-	9	8
5	1	÷	2	=	×	8	2	1	5
1	6	=	1	5	×	8	=	3	5
9	8	0	2	=	2	+	8	1	1

In this puzzle, these letters are used to represent numbers:

C = 3   D = 4   E = 5   F = 6   G = 7   H = 8

Now, try doing the following calculations in your head without writing anything down until you have the final answer for each one. Work from left to right along each line, starting with the first letter and then doing each maths operation in turn. Write each answer as a letter too.

1)   C + G – H × D = ...

2)   H – E × C – D = ...

3)   E × G – G ÷ G = ...

Without drawing on the page, can you help the superhero through the maze below? Keep count of the numbers you pass on the way and write down the total sum at the end.

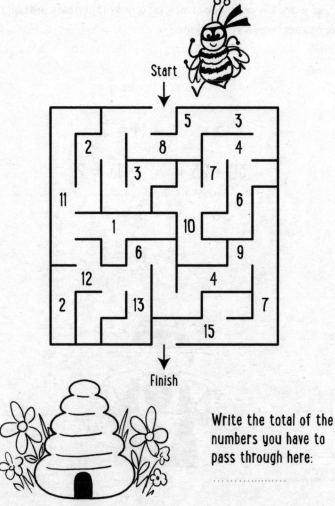

Start

5   3
2   8   4
3   7
11
1   10   6
6   9
12   4
2   13   7
15

Finish

Write the total of the numbers you have to pass through here:

....

Can you help the superhero find the missing number? All of the calculations below are missing the same number. The number is between 1 and 9. If you were to write that number in each of the spaces, all the calculations would give the same result.

Try to work this out without making any written notes. Just fill in the answers when you're done.

.... × .... = ?

5 × .... + 14 = ?

30 + 25 + ... − 13 = ?

8 × .... − 7 = ?

.... × 9 − 14 = ?

Below are some small animal superheroes - mice, beetles and birds all playing on see-saws.

By looking at how they are balanced, can you say which type of animal superhero is the heaviest and which is the lightest?

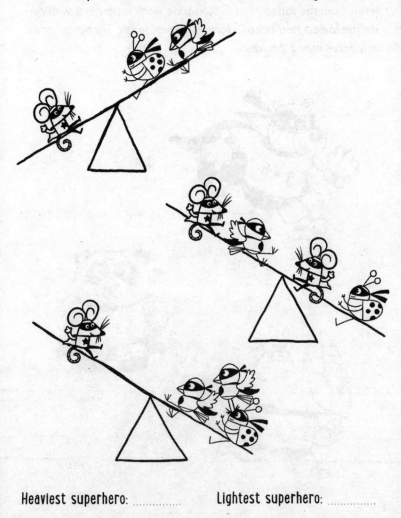

Heaviest superhero: ....   **Lightest superhero:** ....

There are different calculations on these seven superheroes, each of which gives a different result.

Can you sort them into order from lowest result through to highest result? When you have decided on the order, write one letter from the range A to G alongside each superhero, with A for the lowest result and G for the highest result. Try not to make any notes along the way.

....

....

....

8 × 4 ....

19 + 15 ....

23 − 7 ....

6 + 8 + 5 ....

MENTAL MATHS PUZZLE 97

TIME ....

Can you cross out one digit from each of the following calculations to leave a correct calculation?

Here's an example to show you how it works: 14 × ~~2~~3 = 42

If you cross out the '2' it leaves the calculation '14 x 3 = 42', which is correct.

Now try these three yourself. In each one, cross out one digit to make the calculation correct.

a) 101 × 10 = 110

b) 13 × 4 × 12 = 144

c) 50 + 41 + 32 = 78

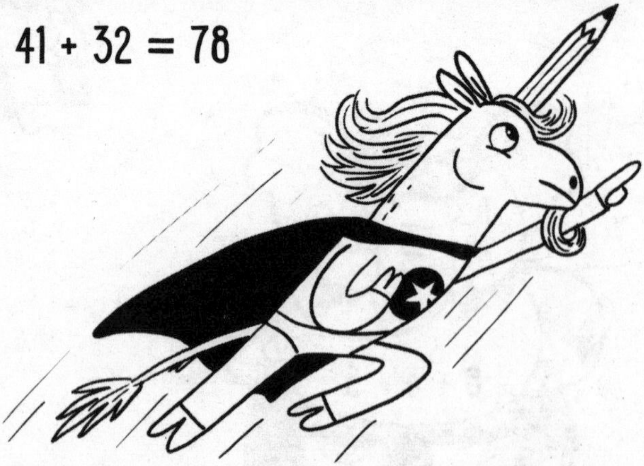

Look carefully at the shapes of these stepping stones.
Can you work out the total number of sides on all of the shapes?
Don't write anything down until you've got the total number,
then put it in the box at the bottom of the page.

There are a total of .... sides

This is not an ordinary dot-to-dot challenge. First, you have to work out which five numbers belong to the same times table. There must be exactly five numbers. Then, without joining the dots, can you work out what shape the joined dots would create? Write your answer in the space at the bottom of the page, then join the dots to see if you're right.

Shape: ....

This is a tricky mental arithmetic task!

The aim is to solve each of the following calculations and add up their results — all without writing anything down. To do this, you'll need to remember the total of each calculation as you're doing the next one.

For example, if there were three calculations, and they resulted in 3, 14 and 8, then you would add these up to get 25.

$$3 + 5 + 2$$
$$4 + 2 + 4$$
$$4 \times 3$$
$$14 - 7$$
$$2 \times 3 \times 3$$

Write your final total here: ....

MENTAL MATHS PUZZLE 101 ⟶

⏲ TIME ....

Each line of this puzzle contains two calculations. In most cases, the calculation on the left-hand side gives the same result as the calculation on the right-hand side.

On two of the lines, however, the left-hand and right-hand sides give different results. Can you find those two lines without making any written notes? When you're done, circle your answers.

7 x 3	and	15 + 6
99 ÷ 9	and	22 – 10
55 + 44	and	111 – 12
63 + 32	and	120 – 25
4 + 44	and	12 x 4
77 – 55	and	2 x 11
36 ÷ 12	and	9 – 5
30 + 25	and	11 x 5

All
of the
ANSWERS

MENTAL MATHS PUZZLE 1

a)
| 12 | 16 | 20 | 24 |
= 4 times table

b)
| 15 | 18 | 21 | 24 |
= 3 times table

MENTAL MATHS PUZZLE 2

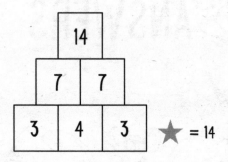

★ = 14

MENTAL MATHS PUZZLE 3

a) 20 – add 3 at each step
b) 28 – minus 2 at each step
c) 27 – add 4 at each step
d) 20 – minus 10 at each step

MENTAL MATHS PUZZLE 4

14 = 7 + 1 + 6
18 = 9 + 4 + 5
21 = 7 + 8 + 6

MENTAL MATHS PUZZLE 5

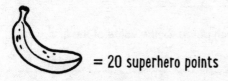 = 20 superhero points

MENTAL MATHS PUZZLE 6

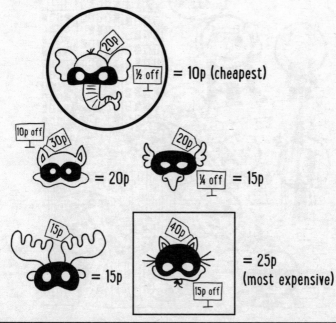

MENTAL MATHS PUZZLE 7

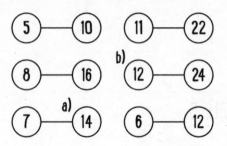

The second number in each pair is 2x the value of the first number.

MENTAL MATHS PUZZLE 8

There are 15 cats.

MENTAL MATHS PUZZLE 9

3 + 5 = 8
4 x 3 = 12
6 + 4 = 10
9 - 2 = 7
1 + 8 = 9

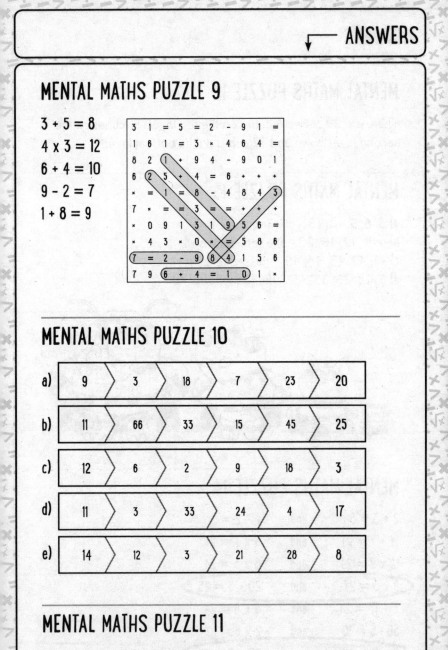

MENTAL MATHS PUZZLE 10

a)	9	3	18	7	23	20
b)	11	66	33	15	45	25
c)	12	6	2	9	18	3
d)	11	3	33	24	4	17
e)	14	12	3	21	28	8

MENTAL MATHS PUZZLE 11

There are 5 squares in total.

MENTAL MATHS PUZZLE 12

There are 29 cubes: 6 cubes on the top layer, 11 cubes on the second layer down and 12 cubes on the bottom layer.

MENTAL MATHS PUZZLE 13

a) 3, 6, 9, 12, 15 – the sequence is +3
b) 4, 8, 12, 16, 20 – the sequence is +4
c) 41, 42, 43, 44, 45 – the sequence is +1
d) 5, 15, 25, 35, 45 – the sequence is +10

MENTAL MATHS PUZZLE 14

2 + 3 = 5	and	7 − 2 = 5
14 + 7 = 21	and	3 x 7 = 21
12 x 2 = 24	and	8 x 3 = 24
9 x 3 = 27	and	20 + 5 = 25
7 + 17 = 24	and	3 x 8 = 24
50 ÷ 5 = 10	and	2 x 5 = 10
8 x 6 = 48	and	40 + 6 = 46
17 + 5 = 22	and	25 − 3 = 22

MENTAL MATHS PUZZLE 15

There are 15 boxes in total, and 5 of them have toys in them.
This gives a fraction of 5/15 boxes having toys in.
The simplest way to write this is 1/3.

MENTAL MATHS PUZZLE 16

a) ? = ×3
b) ? = ×5

MENTAL MATHS PUZZLE 17

There are 27 sides in total.

MENTAL MATHS PUZZLE 18

a) 15 is missing – each number is 3 larger than the previous one.
b) 27 is missing – each number is 2 smaller than the previous one.
c) 13 is missing – each number is 3 larger than the previous one.

MENTAL MATHS PUZZLE 19

5   9   14   20   40

It takes practice to remember numbers, so don't worry if you couldn't remember them all on your first attempt.

MENTAL MATHS PUZZLE 20

$9 \times 1 = 9$

$14 \div 2 = 7$

$24 - 9 = 15$

$40 - 20 = 20$

$4 + 8 = 12$

1	4	÷	2	=	7	=	=	7	1
5	9	0	4	2	2	1	1	+	4
2	1	9	-	1	9	×	=	2	÷
2	0	=	=	2	4	=	4	+	2
1	4	8	0	+	0	-	1	0	=
1	+	-	8	2	9	=	1	×	8
4	4	=	9	=	-	=	2	8	9
4	1	=	1	=	1	0	0	0	1
4	÷	5	6	×	1	9	4	4	2
6	2	1	9	=	9	6	5	-	0

MENTAL MATHS PUZZLE 21

a) $58 = 5 \times 10 + 8$

b) $50 = 5 \times 8 + 10$

MENTAL MATHS PUZZLE 22

a) 6 = 2 and 4
b) 10 = 2 and 8
c) 20 = 4, 7 and 9
d) 26 = 2, 7, 8 and 9

MENTAL MATHS PUZZLE 23

a) 2   3   **4**   6   8   **9**   10   12   14
(the sequence is made up of the 2x and 3x tables)

b) 4   **5**   8   10   12   15   **16**   20   24
(the sequence is made up of the 4x and 5x tables)

c) 3   6   **7**   9   12   14   15   18   **21**
(the sequence is made up of the 3x and 7x tables)

MENTAL MATHS PUZZLE 24

8   12   (14)   19

14 = 5 + 9

MENTAL MATHS PUZZLE 25

a) 1   3   5   7   8   9   11   13
Cross out 8 – each number then increases by 2 at each step

b) 1   5   2   6   3   7   4   5
Cross out the final 5 – the sequence is then +4 -3 +4 -3 +4 -3 +4

c) 1+8   7+2   3+5   5+4   6+3   2+7   8+1   4+5
Cross out 3+5 – all the other sums add up to 9

d) 99   87   75   63   51   41   39   27
Cross out 41 – each number then decreases by 12 at each step

e) 12x3   6x6   3x12   4x9   5x7   1x36   9x4   18x2
Cross out 5x7 – all the other multiplications result in 36

MENTAL MATHS PUZZLE 26

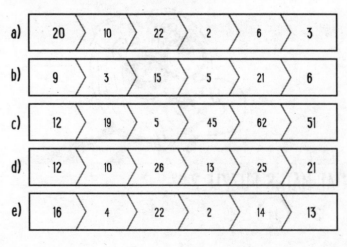

a) 20 > 10 > 22 > 2 > 6 > 3

b) 9 > 3 > 15 > 5 > 21 > 6

c) 12 > 19 > 5 > 45 > 62 > 51

d) 12 > 10 > 26 > 13 > 25 > 21

e) 16 > 4 > 22 > 2 > 14 > 13

MENTAL MATHS PUZZLE 27

The shape is a triangle:

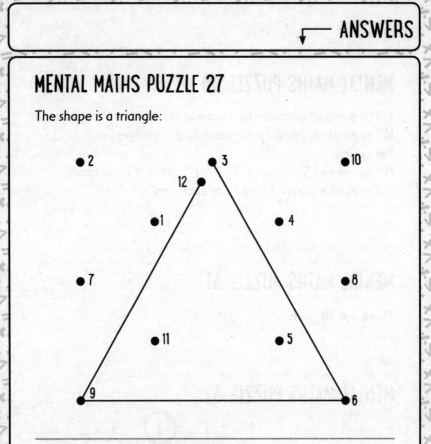

MENTAL MATHS PUZZLE 28

The elephant is the heaviest superhero, the rhino is the lightest.

MENTAL MATHS PUZZLE 29

Answer 1: There are 15 cats – the 5 original cats plus 10 kittens.
Answer 2: There are 9 apples – I had 18 apples to start with, then I ate half (9).

MENTAL MATHS PUZZLE 30

a) The numbers decrease by 11 at each step
b) The numbers go up by 10, down by 20, then repeat this pattern
c) The numbers consist of 1 '1', 2 '2's, 3 '3's, 4 '4's and so on
d) The numbers increase by 12 at each step

MENTAL MATHS PUZZLE 31

There are 18 cards.

MENTAL MATHS PUZZLE 32

2   3   4   6   7   (8)   9

8 was not in the list of numbers.

MENTAL MATHS PUZZLE 33

Answer 1: The five coins are: 50, 50, 5, 2, 1
Answer 2: Four coins: 50, 10, 10, 5
Answer 3: You could have received 10, 10, 10, 1, 1, 1, or 10, 10, 5, 5, 2, 1, since you would have received 33c as change.

MENTAL MATHS PUZZLE 34

a) | 25 | 30 | 35 | 40 | = 5 times table

b) | 36 | 45 | 54 | 63 | = 9 times table

c) | 24 | 27 | 30 | 33 | = 3 times table

MENTAL MATHS PUZZLE 35

5	17	30	82	99
A	C	E	B	D

MENTAL MATHS PUZZLE 36

15 = 2 + 6 + 7
26 = 10 + 12 + 4
30 = 11 + 12 + 7

MENTAL MATHS PUZZLE 37

Answer 1: 2:30pm
Answer 2: 5:30pm
Answer 3: Saturday

MENTAL MATHS PUZZLE 38

1) D (4)
2) F (6)
3) D (4)

MENTAL MATHS PUZZLE 39

1 + 3 = 4	and	5 - 1 = 4
6 x 2 = 12	and	15 - 3 = 12
9 x 4 = 36	and	30 + 6 = 36
5 x 3 = 15	and	18 - 2 = 16
7 + 7 = 14	and	14 x 1 = 14
20 - 10 = 10	and	2 x 5 = 10
13 + 5 = 18	and	12 + 6 = 18
18 - 12 = 6	and	4 x 2 = 8

MENTAL MATHS PUZZLE 40

= 1

= 3

MENTAL MATHS PUZZLE 41

44 is the odd one out.
The three sets of three are:
3x table: 18, 27, 36
5x table: 10, 20, 55
7x table: 14, 49, 56

MENTAL MATHS PUZZLE 42

05:00 | 12 hours later
17:00 = D

19:00 | 1/2 hour later
19:30 = F

12:00 | 3 hours earlier
09:00 = C

11:00 | 3 hours earlier
08:00 = B

16:50

09:00 | 4 hours earlier
05:00 = A

1 hour later
17:50 = E

MENTAL MATHS PUZZLE 43

a) 10 > 6 > 18 > 2 > 3 > 36

b) 13 > 65 > 49 > 62 > 58 > 78

c) 14 > 2 > 12 > 3 > 5 > 55

d) 15 > 3 > 9 > 25 > 5 > 22

e) 9 > 54 > 43 > 51 > 37 > 55

MENTAL MATHS PUZZLE 44

a) $12 \times 2\cancel{6} = 24$ ($12 \times 2 = 24$)
b) $11 + 31 + 5\cancel{1} = 47$ ($11 + 31 + 5 = 47$)
c) $1\cancel{0} \times 7 \times 7 = 49$ ($1 \times 7 \times 7 = 49$)

MENTAL MATHS PUZZLE 45

$3 + 4 = 7$

$5 + 2 = 7$

$3 \times 3 = 9$

$8 \div 2 = 4$

$7 - 4 = 3$

Total $= 30$

MENTAL MATHS PUZZLE 46

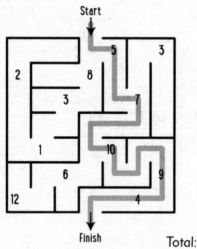

Start

		5	3
2	8		
	3		7
	1		
	10		
	6		9
12			4

Finish

Total: 35

MENTAL MATHS PUZZLE 47

$3 \times 4 = 12$ (B)

$13 + 5 = 18$ (C)

$40 \div 5 = 8$ (A)

$9 \times 3 = 27$ (D)

$5 \times 7 = 35$ (F)

$14 + 18 = 32$ (E)

$8 \times 5 = 40$ (G)

MENTAL MATHS PUZZLE 48

```
        18
     9     9
   4    5    4
```

★ = 4

MENTAL MATHS PUZZLE 49

a) 11, 14, 17, 20, 23 – the sequence is **+3**
b) 25, 34, 43, 52, 61 – the sequence is **+9**
c) 55, 59, 63, 67, 71 – the sequence is **+4**
d) 44, 50, 56, 62, 68 – the sequence is **+6**

MENTAL MATHS PUZZLE 50

There are 24 superheroes in total, and 6 of them are not wearing masks. This gives a fraction of 6/24, which can be simplified to 1/4.

MENTAL MATHS PUZZLE 51

5   8   (5)   9   3   (3)   5

MENTAL MATHS PUZZLE 52

a) 9 = 3 and 6
b) 15 = 3, 4 and 8
c) 20 = 4, 6 and 10
d) 25 = 3, 4, 8 and 10

MENTAL MATHS PUZZLE 53

There are 26 cubes: 5 cubes on the top layer, 9 cubes on the second layer down and 12 cubes on the bottom layer.

MENTAL MATHS PUZZLE 54

a) ? = ×2 − 1
b) ? = ×3 + 1

MENTAL MATHS PUZZLE 55

9	13	32	44	65	107
C	A	E	B	F	D

MENTAL MATHS PUZZLE 56

a) 6, 10, 14, 18, 22, 26, **30** – the sequence is +4
b) 7, 23, 29, 35, 41, 47, **53** – the sequence is +6
c) 19, 27, 35, 43, 51, 59, **67** – the sequence is +8
d) 2, 14, 26, 38, 50, 62, **74** – the sequence is +12
e) 110, 99, 88, 77, 66, 55, **44** – the sequence is –11

MENTAL MATHS PUZZLE 57

a) $25 \div 2 = 12$ remainder **1**
b) $48 \div 7 = 6$ remainder **6**
c) $58 \div 9 = 6$ remainder **4**
d) $67 \div 8 = 8$ remainder **3**

MENTAL MATHS PUZZLE 58

14   (16)   18   20

$16 = 7 + 9$

MENTAL MATHS PUZZLE 59

Answer 1: There are 14 items of cutlery – each plate has 3 next to it, giving 12, and then 2 more are added.

Answer 2: There are 18 people and dogs – 7 dogs plus 7 people, and an additional 4 people.

MENTAL MATHS PUZZLE 60

15	20	26	34	30
11	25	21	29	25
7	22	17	24	21
32	27	23	19	26
27	23	19	24	31

MENTAL MATHS PUZZLE 61

There are 25 vehicles:

MENTAL MATHS PUZZLE 62

a) 2   5   7   8   11   14   17
Cross out 7 – each number then increases by 3 at each step

b) 5x8   4x9   10+30   10x4   20x2   1x40   60-20   8x5
Cross out 4x9 – all the other calculations result in 40

c) 24   4   5   16   8   20   12   10
Cross out 5 – all the other numbers are even (are multiples of 2)

d) 11   24   37   45   50   63   76   89
Cross out 45 – each number then increases by 13 at each step

e) 84   52   21   63   14   70   35   42
Cross out 52 – all the other numbers are multiples of 7

MENTAL MATHS PUZZLE 63

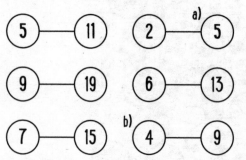

The second number in each pair is formed by multiplying the first number by 2 and then adding 1.

MENTAL MATHS PUZZLE 64

a) 28 〉 19 〉 57 〉 22 〉 11 〉 77

b) 23 〉 62 〉 31 〉 66 〉 22 〉 5

c) 23 〉 46 〉 4 〉 2 〉 16 〉 12

d) 28 〉 14 〉 61 〉 18 〉 48 〉 44

e) 13 〉 51 〉 17 〉 68 〉 34 〉 56

MENTAL MATHS PUZZLE 65

$18 = 1 \times 3 \times 6$
$42 = 7 \times 3 \times 2$
$84 = 7 \times 3 \times 4$

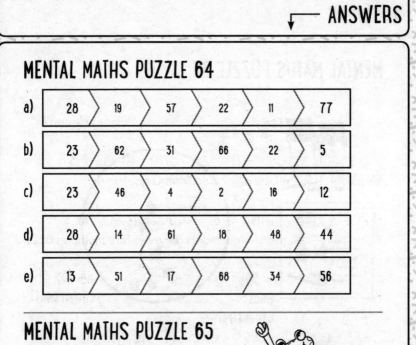

MENTAL MATHS PUZZLE 66

$5 \times 2 = 10$	and	$15 - 5 = 10$
$7 \times 7 = 49$	and	$5 \times 9 = 45$
$3 + 12 = 15$	and	$5 \times 3 = 15$
$6 + 6 = 12$	and	$7 + 5 = 12$
$9 \times 9 = 81$	and	$90 - 9 = 81$
$5 \times 5 = 25$	and	$40 - 15 = 25$
$7 + 32 = 39$	and	$47 - 9 = 38$
$8 \times 3 = 24$	and	$2 \times 12 = 24$

MENTAL MATHS PUZZLE 67

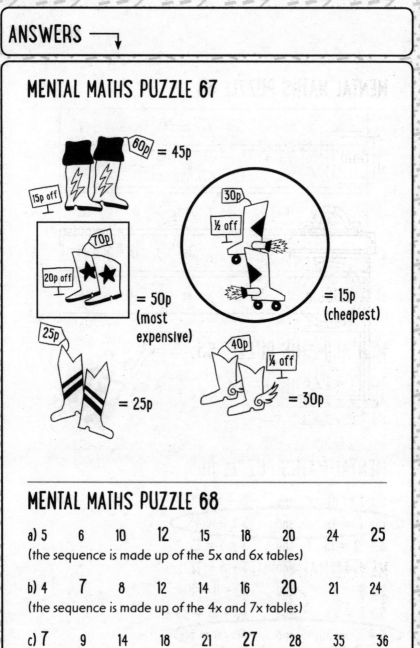

60p, 15p off = 45p

70p, 20p off = 50p (most expensive)

30p, ½ off = 15p (cheapest)

25p = 25p

40p, ¼ off = 30p

MENTAL MATHS PUZZLE 68

a) 5   6   10   **12**   15   18   20   24   **25**
(the sequence is made up of the 5x and 6x tables)

b) 4   **7**   8   12   14   16   **20**   21   24
(the sequence is made up of the 4x and 7x tables)

c) 7   9   14   18   21   **27**   28   35   36
(the sequence is made up of the 7x and 9x tables)

ANSWERS

MENTAL MATHS PUZZLE 69

3am — 60 minutes earlier
2am = A

6pm — 45 minutes later
6.45pm = E

4.30pm — 4 hours later
8.30pm = F

12.15am — 2 hours later
2.15am = B

10:45am — 2 ½ hours later
1.15pm = D

2pm — 90 minutes earlier
12:30pm = C

MENTAL MATHS PUZZLE 70

4   5   (6)   7   8   10   13

6 was not in the original list of numbers.

MENTAL MATHS PUZZLE 71

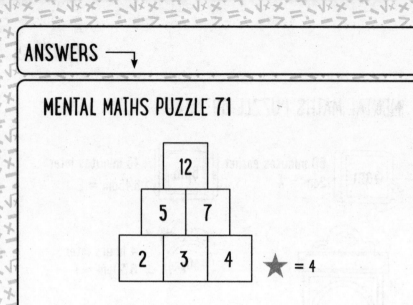

★ = 4

MENTAL MATHS PUZZLE 72

6 + 10 + 2 = 18

3 × 6 = 18

6 × 2 + 6 = 18

25 − 13 + 6 = 18

5 × 6 ÷ 2 + 3 = 18

6 is the missing number in all instances, and all calculations result in 18.

MENTAL MATHS PUZZLE 73

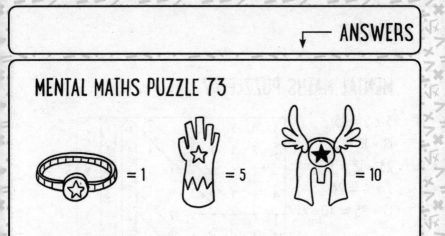

= 1   = 5   = 10

MENTAL MATHS PUZZLE 74

12   8   50   5   100

It takes practice to remember numbers, so don't worry if you couldn't recall them all on your first attempt.

MENTAL MATHS PUZZLE 75

a) 50, 2, 2, 2

b) The fewest number of banknotes is 6: 50, 50, 20, 20, 2, 2

c) Your change of 49b is made up of these banknotes:
20, 20, 5, 2, 2

MENTAL MATHS PUZZLE 76

There are 10 triangles in total.

MENTAL MATHS PUZZLE 77

3 x 5 = 15
19 + 13 = 32
28 - 12 = 16
7 x 4 = 28
15 + 25 = 40

4	0	5	5	1	1	8	0	2	3
2	2	3	9	1	2	1	4	3	×
=	1	1	=	=	1	1	=	=	5
4	4	9	4	5	=	1	5	3	=
×	2	×	+	2	2	1	2	1	1
7	7	1	1	1	=	+	+	+	2
+	-	-	5	5	3	=	5	9	2
5	8	=	×	4	4	=	1	1	3
2	-	3	5	2	-	+	4	2	5
1	6	1	=	2	1	-	8	2	1

MENTAL MATHS PUZZLE 78

a) Each number is equal to the sum of the previous two numbers.

b) The numbers are equal to 12 x 12, 11 x 11, 10 x 10, 9 x 9, 8 x 8, 7 x 7, 6 x 6.

c) Each number is 2x the previous number.

d) The differences between numbers are 2, 3, 4, 5, 6, 7.

MENTAL MATHS PUZZLE 79

14   17   21   (23)

23 = 8 + 15

MENTAL MATHS PUZZLE 80

5 x 3 = 15	and	20 - 5 = 15
9 x 10 = 90	and	110 - 20 = 90
5 x 7 = 35	and	3 x 12 = 36
4 + 24 = 28	and	7 x 4 = 28
19 + 19 = 38	and	15 + 23 = 38
15 + 23 = 38	and	44 - 8 = 36
6 x 6 = 36	and	27 + 9 = 36
90 ÷ 9 = 10	and	40 - 30 = 10

MENTAL MATHS PUZZLE 81

a) 21 = 10 and 11
b) 32 = 8, 10 and 14
c) 37 = 8, 14 and 15
d) 44 = 8, 10, 11 and 15

MENTAL MATHS PUZZLE 82

Answer 1: 6:30am – if I was awake for 15 hours and had lunch after I'd been awake for half that time, that means I had lunch 7 ½ hours after I woke up. If I had a snack two hours after that at 4pm, that means I had lunch at 2pm. 7 ½ hours before that is 6.30am.

Answer 2: Friday. The day before yesterday is 2 days ago, but the day after that is only 1 day ago – so Thursday was only 1 day ago.

Answer 3: 8pm. London is 5 hours ahead of New York City.

MENTAL MATHS PUZZLE 83

32 cubes: 3 cubes on the top layer, 4 cubes on the second layer down, 9 cubes on the third layer down and 16 cubes on the bottom layer.

MENTAL MATHS PUZZLE 84

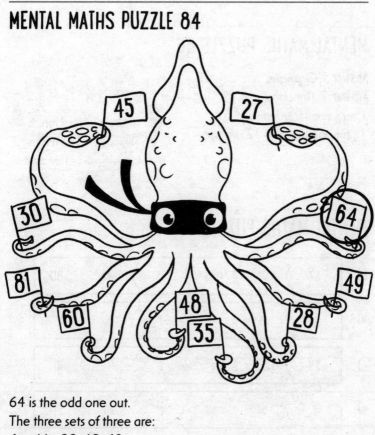

64 is the odd one out.
The three sets of three are:
6x table: 30, 48, 60
7x table: 28, 35, 49
9x table: 27, 45, 81

MENTAL MATHS PUZZLE 85

Answer 1: 9 people got ice creams as a ¼, or 3 of the 12 people didn't want them

Answer 2: 24 pieces of fruit – 3 every day for a total of 21, plus 3 oranges

MENTAL MATHS PUZZLE 86

Answer 1: Oranges
Answer 2: Bananas
There are 10 bananas,
11 pineapples and 12 oranges.

MENTAL MATHS PUZZLE 87

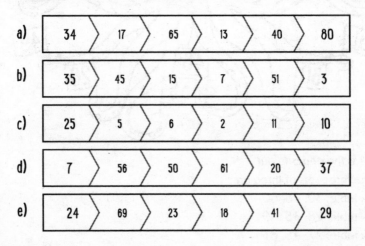

a) 34 > 17 > 65 > 13 > 40 > 80

b) 35 > 45 > 15 > 7 > 51 > 3

c) 25 > 5 > 6 > 2 > 11 > 10

d) 7 > 56 > 50 > 61 > 20 > 37

e) 24 > 69 > 23 > 18 > 41 > 29

MENTAL MATHS PUZZLE 88

2	3	34	50	66	81	97
D	A	B	E	F	G	C

MENTAL MATHS PUZZLE 89

a) 58 is missing – each number is 3 smaller than the previous one

b) 9 is missing – each number is 3 larger than the previous one

c) 33 is missing – each number is 7 larger than the previous one

MENTAL MATHS PUZZLE 90

a) $53 = 10 \times 5 + 2 + 1$

b) $26 = 2 \times 10 + 5 + 1$

c) $21 = 2 \times 5 + 10 + 1$

MENTAL MATHS PUZZLE 91

18 + 2 = 20
35 − 25 = 10
5 x 8 = 40
110 ÷ 10 = 11
96 ÷ 12 = 8

1	1	8	+	2	=	2	2	0	÷
5	3	5	−	2	5	=	1	5	2
1	1	0	÷	1	0	=	1	1	3
0	0	1	1	1	0	9	9	5	0
×	8	0	×	1	=	6	−	4	8
2	2	5	÷	2	÷	2	=	×	1
3	5	0	1	1	5	8	−	9	8
5	1	÷	2	=	×	8	2	1	5
1	6	=	1	5	×	8	=	3	5
9	8	0	2	=	2	+	8	1	1

MENTAL MATHS PUZZLE 92

1) H (8)
2) E (5)
3) D (4)

MENTAL MATHS PUZZLE 93

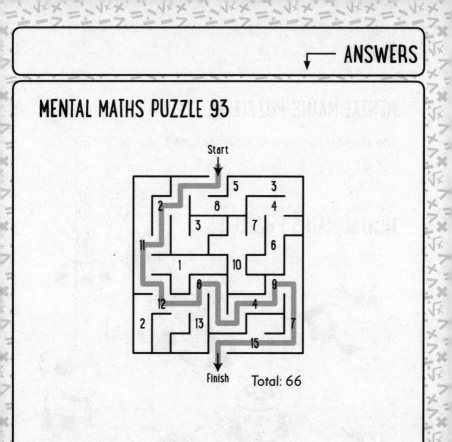

Start

Finish   Total: 66

MENTAL MATHS PUZZLE 94

$7 \times 7 = 49$

$5 \times 7 + 14 = 49$

$30 + 25 + 7 - 13 = 49$

$8 \times 7 - 7 = 49$

$7 \times 9 - 14 = 49$

7 is the missing number in all instances, and all calculations result in 49.

MENTAL MATHS PUZZLE 95

The mouse is the heaviest superhero, the bird is the lightest.

MENTAL MATHS PUZZLE 96

F = 32 — 8×4

5×6 — E = 30

$19 + 15$ — G = 34

A = 9 — $99 \div 11$

B = 16 — $23 - 7$

$3 \times 3 \times 2$ — C = 18

$6 + 8 + 5$ — D = 19

MENTAL MATHS PUZZLE 97

a) $101 \times 10 = 110$ ($11 \times 10 = 110$)
b) $13 \times 4 \times 12 = 144$ ($3 \times 4 \times 12 = 144$)
c) $50 + 41 + 32 = 78$ ($5 + 41 + 32 = 78$)

MENTAL MATHS PUZZLE 98

There are 36 sides in total.

MENTAL MATHS PUZZLE 99

The numbers are part of the 4x table. The shape is a square:

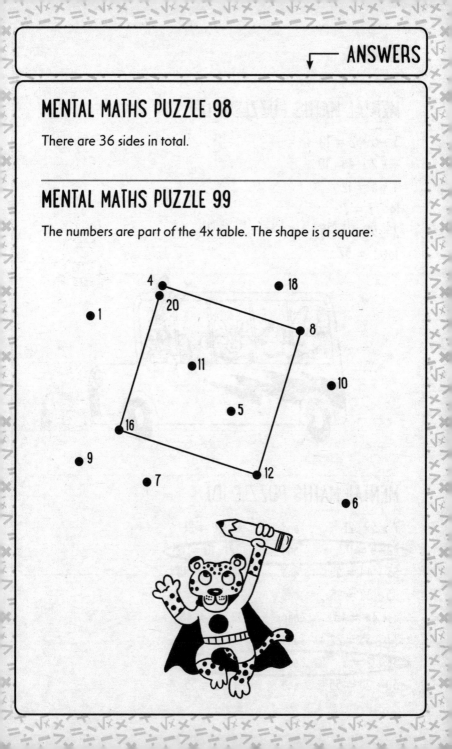

MENTAL MATHS PUZZLE 100

3 + 5 + 2 = 10
4 + 2 + 4 = 10
4 × 3 = 12
14 − 7 = 7
2 × 3 × 3 = 18
Total = 57

MENTAL MATHS PUZZLE 101

7 x 3 = 21	and	15 + 6 = 21
99 ÷ 9 = 11	and	22 − 10 = 12
55 + 44 = 99	and	111 − 12 = 99
63 + 32 = 95	and	120 − 25 = 95
4 + 44 = 48	and	12 x 4 = 48
77 − 55 = 22	and	2 x 11 = 22
36 ÷ 12 = 3	and	9 − 5 = 4
30 + 25 = 55	and	11 x 5 = 55

NOTES
AND
SCRIBBLES

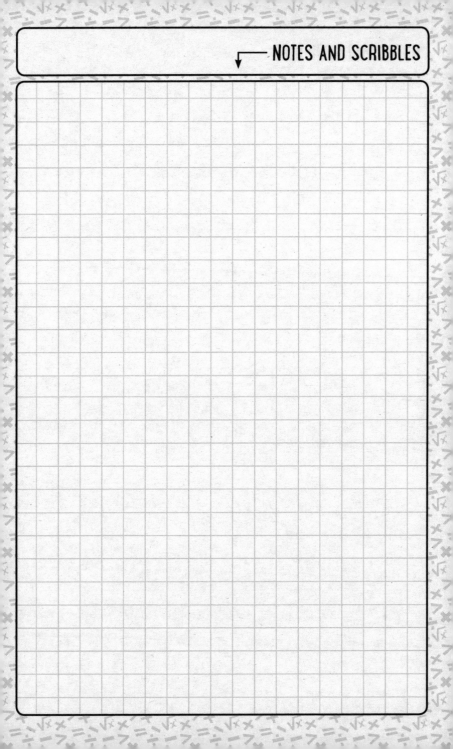

NOTES AND SCRIBBLES →